I0626074

ISBN 978-1-998317-66-0

Cover design by Charlotte Chang.

First Edition: January, 2025

CAT

Cats are small, sneaky animals that have been living with people as pets for thousands of years. They are soft and fluffy, with sharp claws and super sharp senses that help them catch little animals in the wild.

Pet cats are fun to play with and like to do things on their own, but they still love to talk to their humans with meows, purrs, and funny movements.

Cats can see really well in the dark, which makes them amazing hunters at night. They're like tiny, furry ninjas!

🧬 Scientific Name: Felis catus

🏠 Habitat: Your couch; wild cats live in forests, grasslands, and deserts.

🥛 Food: Carnivore—eats small animals like mice and birds, or commercial cat food.

⏳ Lifespan: 12–18 years (domesticated).

📏 Length: 58–76.2 cm (including tail).

⚖️ Weight: 4.1 - 5.4 kg on average, depending on breed.

Did you know?

In ancient Egypt, cats were worshiped as sacred animals, and harming a cat was considered a serious crime!

ELEPHANT

Elephants are the biggest animals that live on land, and you can spot them easily by their long trunks, huge floppy ears, and thick gray skin.

They live in families called herds, which are led by the oldest female. Elephants are super smart, have amazing memories, and love spending time with each other.

Their trunks are like magical tools—they use them to drink water, eat food, and even toss dust on their backs to stay cool. Elephants eat tons of plants every day and help nature by spreading seeds when they poop.

🧬 Scientific Name: Loxodonta africana (African elephant),
                    Elephas maximus (Asian elephant)

🏡 Habitat: Grasslands, forests, and savannas in Africa and Asia.

🍽 Food: Herbivore—eats grass, fruits, leaves, and bark.

⏳ Lifespan: 60–70 years in the wild.

📏 Length: 5.5–7.5 meters.

⚖ Weight: 2,000–6,350 kg.

Did you know?

Elephants are excellent swimmers and can use their trunk as a snorkel when crossing deep water!

DOG

Dogs are smart and loyal animals that have been our best friends for thousands of years! They love being around people and can live in groups, both in the wild and at home. There are so many kinds of dogs, from tiny Chihuahuas you can carry in your hand to giant Great Danes as big as a pony!

Dogs have amazing noses that can sniff out things like lost people, hidden treats, and even help doctors find out if someone is sick. They truly are amazing furry friends!

🧬 Scientific Name: Canis lupus familiaris

🏡 Habitat: Your living room; though wild dogs like dingoes live in forests, savannas, and deserts.

🍴 Food: Omnivore—eats meat, vegetables, and dog food made from both.

⏳ Lifespan: 10–15 years (depending on breed).

📏 Length: 60–110 cm (varies greatly by breed).

⚖️ Weight: 1.5–90 kg (depending on breed).

Did you know?

A dog's sense of smell is so strong that it can detect a teaspoon of sugar in two Olympic-sized swimming pools!

RABBIT

Rabbits are cute, fluffy animals with long ears and strong back legs. Their big ears help them hear danger, and their strong legs help them hop away really fast!

Rabbits love to munch on grass, leafy greens, and yummy veggies. They have lots of baby bunnies very quickly, which is why there are so many of them!

In the wild, rabbits dig tunnels called burrows to stay safe from predators. Pet rabbits are friendly and love spending time with their owners. They make great furry friends!

🧬 Scientific Name: Oryctolagus cuniculus

🏡 Habitat: Grasslands, forests, and domesticated environments.

🍴 Food: Herbivore—eats grasses, leafy greens, hay, and vegetables.

⏳ Lifespan: 8–12 years (domesticated).

📏 Length: 35–50 cm.

⚖️ Weight: 1–4.5 kg (depending on breed).

Did you know?

Rabbits' teeth never stop growing, so they have to chew on things constantly to keep them from getting too long!

LION

Lions are powerful carnivores that live in the grassy lands of Africa. People often call them the "king of the jungle" because of their powerful roar and royal look.

Unlike most big cats, lions live in family groups called prides. Male lions have big, fluffy manes that protect them during fights, while the females are the best hunters and catch food for the group.

Lions are at the very top of the food chain, which means they help keep nature balanced by hunting other animals. They're truly the kings of their world!

🧬 Scientific Name: Panthera leo

🏡 Habitat: Grasslands and savannas in Africa and a small population in India.

🍽️ Food: Carnivore—eats zebras, antelopes, and other large animals.

⏳ Lifespan: 10–14 years in the wild.

📏 Length: 1.6–2.5 meters (excluding tail).

⚖️ Weight: 120–190 kg (males are larger).

Did you know?

Rabbits' teeth never stop growing, so they have to chew on things constantly to keep them from getting too long!

KANGAROO

Kangaroos are big, bouncy animals that live in Australia and are famous for their super strong legs that let them hop really far.

Female kangaroos have a special pouch to carry their babies, called joeys, until the joeys are big enough to explore on their own.

Kangaroos eat plants like grass and shrubs, and their long tails help them keep their balance while hopping. They love hanging out together in groups called mobs and can hop as fast as 71 km per hour—faster than most cars in a neighborhood!

🧬 Scientific Name: Macropus species
🏡 Habitat: Grasslands, forests, and deserts in Australia.
🍴 Food: Herbivore—eats grass, leaves, and shrubs.
⏳ Lifespan: 6–8 years in the wild; up to 20 years in captivity.
📏 Length: 1.2–1.8 meters (including tail).
⚖️ Weight: 18–90 kg.

Did you know?

Kangaroos can't move their back legs independently—they always hop or use both legs together!

BEAR

Bears are big, strong animals that can live in all kinds of places, like forests and snowy tundras. They eat all sorts of things, including plants, fish, and small animals, which makes them great at finding food anywhere they go.
Some bears, like polar bears, are amazing swimmers, while others, like grizzlies, can run really fast.
Bears have thick, fluffy fur that keeps them cozy in the cold, and when winter comes, many of them take long naps called hibernation to stay warm and save energy.
They're like nature's sleepy giants!

🧬 Scientific Name: Ursidae family
🏘️ Habitat: Forests, mountains, tundras, and Arctic regions.
🪣 Food: Omnivore—eats berries, fish, honey, and meat.
⏳ Lifespan: 20–30 years in the wild.
📏 Length: 1.5–3 meters.
⚖️ Weight: 40–700 kg, depending on the species.

Did you know?

Polar bears have black skin –
even though their fur looks
white, polar bears' skin is
actually black to absorb heat
from the sun.

HORSE

Horses are strong and fast animals that have been helping people for thousands of years. They can run far, carry heavy things, and even help farmers by pulling plows. Horses love living in groups called herds, where they make friends and stick together. They "talk" to each other with neighs, snorts, and body movements.
With their speed, strength, and smarts, horses are amazing helpers and wonderful friends to humans!

🧬 Scientific Name: Equus ferus caballus
🏡 Habitat: farms; wild horses live in grasslands, plains, and deserts.
🍽️ Food: Herbivore—eats grass, hay, and grains.
⏳ Lifespan: 25–30 years.
📏 Height: 1.4–1.8 meters.
⚖️ Weight: 380–1,000 kg, depending on the breed.

Did you know?

Horses can sleep standing up, thanks to a special locking system in their legs!

DEER

Deer are gentle, graceful animals with long legs, and the males grow antlers that fall off and grow back every year. They live in forests and meadows, munching on plants while always staying on the lookout for danger.
Deer can run super fast to escape predators, and baby deer, called fawns, are born with spotted coats that help them hide in the grass and stay safe.
Deer are amazing at blending into nature!

🧬 Scientific Name: Cervidae

🏡 Habitat: Forests, grasslands, and mountains.

🍽️ Food: Herbivore—eats leaves, grass, and fruits.

⌛ Lifespan: 10–15 years in the wild.

📏 Height: 0.8–1.5 meters at the shoulder.

⚖️ Weight: 30–300 kg, depending on the species.

Did you know?

Male deer grow new antlers every year, and antlers are one of the fastest-growing bones in the animal world.

HEDGEHOG

Hedgehogs are tiny animals with spiky backs covered in stiff quills. When they get scared, they roll up into a little ball to keep themselves safe.

Hedgehogs sleep during the day and come out at night to look for yummy bugs and worms to eat. They have super good hearing and a strong nose that helps them find food in the dark. Some people even keep hedgehogs as pets because they're so cute and fun to watch!

🧬 Scientific Name: Erinaceinae.

🏡 Habitat: Grasslands, forests, and deserts.

🍴 Food: Omnivore—eats insects, worms, fruits, and small animals.

⏳ Lifespan: 4–7 years in the wild; up to 10 years in captivity.

📏 Length: 14–30 cm.

⚖️ Weight: 0.4–1.2 kg.

Did you know?

Hedgehogs can have up to 7,000 tiny quills on their backs to keep them safe from predators!

COW

Cows are gentle animals that love to eat grass and can live on farms or in the wild. They have big, round bodies, a calm and friendly nature, and they give us milk to drink.
Cows spend most of their day munching on grass in fields, and their amazing stomachs have four parts to help them digest their food.
They also have a great memory and can remember faces, places, and even other cows!

🪶 **Scientific Name:** Bos taurus
🏡 **Habitat:** farms; wild cattle live in grasslands and forests.
🍴 **Food:** Herbivore—eats grass, hay, and grains.
⏳ **Lifespan:** 15–20 years.
📏 **Length:** 2.5–3 meters.
⚖️ **Weight:** 450–1,800 kg, depending on the breed.

Did you know?

Cows form close friendships with other cows and can get stressed when separated from their buddies.

SQUIRREL

Squirrels are fast, clever little animals that love climbing trees. They use their big, fluffy tails to help them balance, keep warm in the cold, and even steer when they jump. Squirrels eat nuts, seeds, and fruits, and they hide extra food for winter—sometimes they forget where they put it, and new trees grow! They're amazing jumpers and can leap from branch to branch.
Squirrels are also really smart and can figure out how to get to tricky snacks!

🧬 Scientific Name: Sciuridae.
🏠 Habitat: Forests, parks, and urban areas with trees.
🍼 Food: Omnivore—eats nuts, seeds, fruits, and small insects.
⏳ Lifespan: 6–12 years in the wild.
📏 Length: 20–30 cm (not including the tail).
⚖️ Weight: 0.5–1.5 kg.

Did you know?

Squirrels can find food they buried months earlier by using their incredible memory and sense of smell!